ABOUT THE AUTHOR

Tim Wells has cultivated a laugh that's more like a caress. He walks properly. He does not slouch, shuffle or stumble about. He knows that wide, floating trousers are only good for wearing on a veranda with a cocktail in your hand.

PRAISE FOR TIM WELLS

'London poetry landmark'
The Times Literary Supplement

'Working class hero'
The Morning Star

'Thug'
NME, 18th July 1984

ALSO BY TIM WELLS

POETRY

A Man Can Be A Drunk Sometimes, But A Drunk Can't Be A Man (Donut Press, 2001)

If You Can Read This You're Too Close (Donut Press, 2003)

Boys' Night Out in the Afternoon (Donut Press, 2005)

Rougher Yet (Donut Press, 2009)

Keep the Faith (Blackheath Books, 2014)

Everything Crash
Tim Wells

Penned in the Margins

LONDON

PUBLISHED BY PENNED IN THE MARGINS
Toynbee Studios, 28 Commercial Street, London E1 6AB
www.pennedinthemargins.co.uk

First published 2015

Printed in the United Kingdom by TJ International.

ISBN
978-1-908058-21-8

ACKNOWLEDGEMENTS

Acknowledgements are due to the editors of the following publications in which some of these poems first appeared: *Brogue, Broken Wine, Clarity, Cont, Counterfeit Crank, The Daily Bugle, Dripping, Dwang, Freedom, Inside View, In Their Own Words* (Salt Publishing, 2012), *Junior Gazette, The London Column, Magma Poetry, Morning Star, The Moth, N16, New Left Project, New Trespass, Nutsack, Onion, Pen Pusher Magazine, Poetry* (Chicago), *The Prague Review, Push, Ration Book, Snatch, Street Sounds, SugarApe, The Tally Ho, The Weekend On Sunday* and *Yeast.*

Nine of the poems collected here first appeared in the pamphlet *Keep the Faith* (Blackheath Books, 2014).

'The Column Inches' and 'WPC Lucy Sheridan' first appeared in a limited edition pamphlet, *The Column Inches*, published by Sick Fly Publications to mark the thirty-fifth anniversary of the death of Mary Millington in 2014.

I WOULD LIKE TO RAISE A GLASS TO:

Angela Mao Ying, Ingrid Pitt, Jason King, Andy Ching, Ashna Sarkar, Phill Jupitus, Roxanne Escobales, Squire, Squire, Sarah, Jan, Clare Pollard, Jane Yeh, I Roy, The Sweeney, Cockney Rejects, Phil Silvers, Geraint Hughes, Aileen Cho, Ted Taylor, Adina Edwards, Warren Oates, Bobbie Gentry, Melisser Elliott, Mustang Sally, Lo Lieh, Hasina Begum, Aza Shadenova, Major Lance, Mistah Brown, Tim P, Arms House Champian, Suzi Quatro, Maggie Ryan, Helen Mort, Sleaford Mods, Jan Wacław Machajski, Ian Duhig, Sir Percy Blakeney, Sugar Pie DeSanto, Todd Moore, Michael Curran, Lucy Parsons, Isaac Bashevis Singer, MiG 21, unruly breasts, the Jones, Harry Champion, Mrs Elswood, Rudolf Rocker, Niall O'Sullivan, the new Number Two, Emma Peel, Sarah Lund, Bang Said the Gun, Rhoda Dakar, the mice on the mouse organ, Adebisi, Hannah Lowe, all the young dudes, Ted Lewis, Laurie Cunningham, James Herbert, Cheryl B, Reiko Ike, Terry Sneed, PP Snatch, girls with price tags on the soles of their shoes, Johnny Alucard, Anna and Nick, Liang Shan Po, Fred Voss, Barry Cryer, George Smiley, Salena Godden, Barry Brown, Cody Jarrett, General Urko, Imogen Salt, Mary Hooligan, Gunter and Lucille Toody, Koko Taylor, Rollerball Rocco, pie and mash, Serious Drinking, Isaac Babel, Nick Tesco, Ogami Itto, Vimto, Miki Berenyi, Hard As Nails, Tog, Snuff, Nigel Benn, Junjo Lawes, Destiny, Melody, Harmony, Symphony and Rhapsody, Mouldy Old Dough, Castle of Owls, UK Bubblers, Jack Underpants, Angel Delight, Arthur Morrison, the Hoxton Creeper, lager top, Karen Black, Ring Lardner, Ranking Slackness, Delinquent Girl Boss, Junior Soul, Cesar Romero, Penlingtons all, Flannery O'Connor, Jenni Fagan, Asta, June Millington, Nina Baden-Semper, The Gymslips, Doug and Dinsdale, Joel Loya, Victor Serge, Jennifer Wong, Barrington Levy, Scratch the Upsetter, Cesca, Johnny Reggae, The Mighty Two, Charles Middleton, Sven Hassel, and the grave next to Arch Stanton.

CONTENTS

For Beatrice Pons

Everything Crash

Hoxton Market Forces

A piano teeters on the edge
of the top floor, Balfron Tower.
The seconds before it plummets,
the electricity of coming rent-rises
runs through the assembled tenants.

Gone are the aerosoled (classic)
cock and balls, paintbrushed football teams.
'Artists' are the rats that herald the plague.

A stabbed local lad's claret
is Tweeted, selfied and playlisted;
the Jobcentre now a bar
where trust funds flaunt their edge:
irony is when they don't have the balls
to flick two fingers to our face,
yet they're two fingers still.

The piano powers down
as our rents soar up.
The crash is a certain music:
a cacophony of notes. Bank notes.

The Early Throes

You realise, the fifth time she uses it,
it's the pet name she's given you.
You're walking along Oxford Street.

She takes your hand
and you have to hold the book you're carrying
in front of your groin
to mask the rising tightness in your stride.

The book is Apuleius' *The Golden Ass*
and you march it from Topshop to American Apparel.
The title and your gait make a Swedish tourist laugh.

You name the shade on her lips, dress size and shoe.
You walk past shops and picture her
in outfits that catch your eye.
This new found attention to women's fashion worries you.

You start to eat differently — wasabi peas, rocket —
and become aware of soya milk.
You wake up in the morning singing 'Can I Get a Witness'.

You think less about the swish of her thighs
and the give of her breast,
but more of the splash of her laugh

and how her smile breaks like a sunrise
from the black of her hair
and the dark of your day.

Together Again

My dad would arrive at breakfast
with a pencil behind his ear.
He'd draw a face on his boiled egg
which often resembled Philip Larkin.

"They fuck you up, your mum and dad"
he would intone. "They may not mean to,
but they do." Then, looking at me,
he'd crack his spoon on Larkin's skull,

shatter his pate and cram toast soldiers
in the eggy cranium — eating the yolk,
leaving a deep crevasse. I once said
the bald head looked like the anarchist Ian Bone.

With spoon poised, my dad yelled "Bash the rich!"
then smashed the soft-boiled crown.

My Sad Hooligans

After Thom Gunn

One by one they slip to birds,
curries, darkness.
Saturday night never lives to its promise,
though a nod and a wink sometimes does.

These men we have been
and could have been.
Wasted force spent with passion;
initials pissed against the wall.

The bully of the supermarket stockroom
sleeps drunk in the Boogie Lounge.
He wakes with a start
as the mirrorball explodes.

In Praise of Chimène Suleyman

Behind me
on the top deck of the 67 bus
two Turkish girls
dressed for a night out
talk about life
since leaving school
the other side of summer.
One works in Westfield,
the shopping centre
that's our Olympic legacy.
The other's started college
but is enjoying it not much.
"I have to go," she explains.
"My dad's a Marxist.
He says I have to be educated
'cos the bourgeoisie treat
the proletariat like mice."
Her friend nods and says,
"He's worked in shops, your dad."

R. Dean Taylor

How annoying that those who lived a sedentary life ~
slippers, supper and Sunday papers ~ and had no truck
with dybbuks, table-tapping nor the death herald
spontaneous smashing of a plate set for family dinner,

how annoying to find themselves not at rest,
haunting their old haunts, that the mysteries prevail.
Worse yet, seen only by freaky mediums, goths
and contributors to women's magazines.

The Middle Class in the Launderette as Pandas at the Zoo

At first they're wide-eyed
and insufferably cute;
the light is more than expected,
surroundings unfamiliar.
They tread gingerly,
touch machines
and wash-baskets gently.
The soap powder box
might as well be
an ice block
containing pear chunks.
Them working out
where the coins go
will be shared on YouTube
by Japanese girls
for months;
their precious
middle-class faces of awe
memed, t-shirted and tea-towelled.
They actually read
washing instructions on labels,

use fabric softener
and turn up without
the correct coins.
O the joy
of the *what to do?*
till the Turkish lady
sorts them change,
explains a service wash.
I can't afford the zoo these days,
but I surely rinse my smalls.

Kuu

I knew she was the Finn for me
when walking across Springfield Park
in the dark from the pub
she made a lunge at me, planted a kiss,
pointed to the heavens and exclaimed
excitedly, "a shitting star."

Baby Workout

Get dressed, get blessed
Try to be a success
Bob Dylan, 'Subterranean Homesick Blues'

How he got here doesn't matter: the raw talent, the hours
of practice, the racism; the mob that gets you breaks
but never lets you rest; the hits, the girls, the hangers-on.
Even if tonight it's just the uppers keeping him upright,
when the spotlight hits, he's on his own, all else fades
and Mr Excitement is king of the room. Horns punch,
drums jab and hook, he ducks, weaves, *that* voice soars,
lifts 'em up and knocks 'em clean out. Dancing
into centre-stage, he throws his jacket over his shoulder,
arches back, knees bent — sweat soaks his silk shirt.
Flipping forward, rolling hips, shoes shuffling in a blur,
if he undid the fly of his shark-skin trousers, it'd take a bite.
He knows, as the girls tear his clothes and he's ankle deep in
                                    lingerie,
it's important not to dress as who you are, but who you want to be.

Ryoko Naitoh Writes a Song

As a girl
she always went
to the bottom
of the dressing-up box.

Her first word
was "クソガキ."
Her first English,
"Fuku you!"

Her guitar taller than she,
but never as mighty.

The music:
the slaps of Hiroko Nagata
bemoaning the lot
of Japanese women.

The words:
stars set ablaze
by a punch.
The page is my face.

Born to Rule

There's an awkward moment early in a DJ's set;
you're dropping class choons, no one's drunk,
no one's dancing. Do you drop sounds
everyone knows and loves, but are cheesy,
or do you use this time to rinse the obscure records
you don't normally get to bust — the killers?
Well, you save them for when it all gets
Lord of the Flies. Me, I don't stress it.
They're my records, they're playing loud
and behind the decks no one can see my tumescence.

Out of the Blue

There are those for whom moving house is all so many pennies in a jar: it'll all amount to something. I am more the alchemist: slowly, but not surely, making the mundane something precious.

Just as it is several floors above the street, my new flat is in nearly every way better than my old ground floor one, all except for the cheap plastic toilet seat that wasn't even bolted to the bowl. I took a dislike to it even before I'd started sliding left, right and front and back every time I eased myself; sat there a-flipping and a-flopping in some kinda kooky Pan's People routine.

No big deal; I now live amidst a jangle of pound shops and determined to purchase and attach a brand new model. I spotted a real bobby dazzler: clear resin filled with silver glitter. I liked it. It had a certain 1974 'gay bloke in a glam rock band' quality but did it give the message that I wanted to send, to ladies especially? So I got plain wood. No mistaking that. This, however, soon broke; too much cheesecake too soon?

Of course there'd been second thoughts, and my framed portraits of Ingrid Pitt and the sheer number of reggae singles would surely choke any doubts about my dance moves raised by this, admittedly, exuberant toilet seat. I returned and purchased the glitter that could, perhaps, handle the weight of my pretensions.

The bathroom is the one place where we truly relax. We are confronted with the true selves we love, loathe or try to avoid. Both seat and lid moulded stardust! My life has plopped into the plush.

I've taken to hot, foamy baths with Roxy Music's *Greatest Hits* pumping on the stereo. Lathered with scented foam, I wonder about Brian Ferry looking through an old picture frame. Heavy is the head that wears the crown, Thane of Bathwater.

Us skinhead types aren't known for our decadence (Desmond excluded that is). Even now I'm more Coal Tar than Imperial Leather. Citrus mouth wash has appeared in my bathroom cabinet. I've even started using it twice daily, according to directions.

Outside, Ermine Street walks backwards to the gilt and butchery of Londinium; then, as now, my manor blinged-up vermin. My street is a busy one, a dirty one, a loud one. Police cars scream past, sirens forcing themselves in. It's not the noise I object to. It's the urgency. I'm all for the fight against crime, but surely it can be done in a more Sherlock Holmes and gentlemanly languid manner?

Iniquity is a mire into which we are sinking, or a briar catching at us with thorns. I forget which, although I note that these encompass both descent and ascension. The road to hell may be paved with good intentions, but the road to Whitechapel is laid far less savoury.

The Commercial Tavern, once a trysting place for East End homosexualists, is now frequented by 'artists' and the like. I work around the corner and am there for the lock in. For all its bustling traffic, Commercial Street crawls slower than most of London. Painters whine, beer flows, brasses ply their trade; much the same as in the Ripper's heyday.

I am introduced to, and shake hands with, the new landlord; tall, louche, pastel open-necked yet masculine shirt, sovereigns all heads, blonde flipped hair… no less than Brian Ferry in negative!

The police speed past, the prostitutes splash.

Version

My girl Jessie is from a family of dockers.
If you're wondering if she swears like one,
she does. It was from her foghorn mouth
that I first heard Michael Smith,
and you know how it is with teenage lads:
if a girl is passionate you want to know all about it.
She played me 'Trainer' from the tail end of an NME cassette.

'for it was de firs time in me life
a really feel fi seh something
an a couldn bring out nuttin

so a jus walk'

That hard yard voice rumbled from the deck;
so unlike ours, but it spoke to us all the same.
It's no accident reggae boomed from our teenage bedrooms;
Jamaica was only as far as next door.
When people wake up, they find their own speech.
We were shook awake: no jobs, no money, no future.
Hackney, Detroit, Johannesburg or Kingston JA.
Both dub slates and police batons have a beat all their own.

As the punks sang
tell you the truth I can't afford to run away, from the UK
Mikey's words were fingers balling to a fist,
an incendiary device, the static on the filth's radio,
braziers on the picket line, piss stains on brutalist concrete,
the look passed from eye to eye at the dole queue.
Not no Shelley *Sew seeds but let no tyrants reap*
but he and we knew — forward ever, backward never.

Stoic Youth

The trick was to go to the music room en route and pluck three strands from a violin bow. When wrapped around your palm, the horsehair would bite as you were caned and cause you to bleed. At that stage you might get sympathy — teachers are afeared of blood — or the Head might continue, depending on your infraction.

Another ploy was to stuff a comic down your trousers. For less serious offences you were bent over; though not being public school, we weren't bare-arsed pervy whacked. If your subterfuge was discovered, you were given an extra six.

Most important was that you show no emotion. Since then I've brought a blank face to pain, shame and when my education is mocked.

Bidaaye

Eating curry with Hasina
when three Brick Lane girls walk in,
look to her then me, quizzically.

They question her; not in the usual Sylheti, but Bengali.
When Bengali comes out it's time to worry —
it's like getting a letter from the Council.

"English please," says Hasina. "I'm with my friend."
"We are your people," throws out the first girl.
Hasina looks to me then turns to them: "No,
you are why my family left home to find home."

Small Axe

She is beautiful and slight;
not weak, but finely turned,

much as a precise pair of scales
will balance all that is put upon them

~ first this way, then that ~
and then speak true; the way

a leisurely man cups
a welcome pair of breasts

and deliberates on the fluctuations
of fortune that may be his fate.

Red Cavalry

Saturday night afters and this gaggle enters:
haughty and drunk, that watchable cocktail
of *I am the best thing here, I am nervous.*
The girls pose by the mirror and unbutton coats.

"Russians," spits my friend Aza: she grew up
speaking it. The blokes are at the bar, trying
to buy the fancy drinks that the girls won't get
in an after-hours. Aza peers on. Her view
of contemporary culture is one I always welcome.

"Russian girls, you always see them with fat men."
She prods me in my ample gut. "English men, you see
with fat girls."
           And you, Aza? I query. "Me? I am
from Kyrgyzstan. I own all you bitches." And so she does.

A Little Less Conversation

Those who cannot remember the past are condemned to repeat it.
George Santayana

Framed above my toilet:
a photo of Vegas-era Elvis.
Not everyone gets the joke.

The Monkey Time

And then the music begins to play,
Automatically you're on your way.
Are you ready?

Major Lance, 'The Monkey Time'

Another Saturday night,
another mess of people
dancin' to choons
from the all killer/no filler box.
This one girl shuffles up,
asks for "summink by The Contours."
I'm happy to oblige,
more so as she gets to shaking it.
She asks a few more and gets them.
Tells me her name,
that she's from Camberwell.
I must be happy drunk
'cos I don't even pull a face at that.
She works "in the public sector."
Takes me a while to winkle out
just what that is: something about
an office, paperwork

and targets, targets, targets.
Half listening and cueing up Major Lance,
I pull a sympathy face.
"Do you have targets?" she asks.
Eyes that wide and a mouth that open
deserve an answer, so I tell her
to make the biggest pair of tits in the room jiggle.
She leans close and plants a kiss on my cheek.

Mudies Mood

The Rhythm Rulers, *Mudies Mood*, Moodisc (1970)

There was an anticipation in dropping needle to groove — coming home on the bus, album on lap, looking at the sleeve. *Mudies Mood* had a *chinee* girl on the cover. My teenage years were reggae and kung fu films; this one record was talking direct.

With the interweb, discovery is easy nowadays. When I was young we had to search for sounds and for what we needed to know about producers and singers — album notes gleaned, xeroxed 'zines poured over, blurred pictures pondered. The lack of information helped build legends.

I didn't know all the tracks. Dennis Walks' 'The Drifter' was certainly reason enough for my buying; I'd first got that as a Crab seven from Reggae Paul at Camden Market. I'd beaten a lad called Tim P to the punch on that one — Tim and I have been mates ever since.

Harry Mudie was known for tough *riddims*. Rhythm, at a time we were actually starting to get somewhere with girls — cinemas, parties and sometimes bedrooms. Real girls, who drank, danced and sometimes desired us too. All that rhythm to move to.

Not just that, Mudie had a sweep of strings also. The rush of them, blasting from the stereo, was intense. Winston Wright chopping keyboard... what a rush. Some things you never forget, some things you never want to forget. Let me tell you boy... here comes I Roy!

The Winger

I'd not thought of him for years.
Not one of the clever kids, yet
no idiot, and too nice a lad
to be a bully — but good enough

at football they all wanted to know him.
Never dressed too smart:
worn jumper and plimsolls.
On the football pitch he became himself.

Holding the left wing, when the ball
came to him he'd dribble, run, fly.
Body... sleek, not gawky,
red jersey more standard than bunting.

He knocked plenty of goals in,
but with him it seemed the joy
was outpacing everyone, ball at his feet.
When he left school no one ever saw him again.

A Quitter Never Wins

A retort to critical theory

It's heart-warming:
my troublesome daughter
is tapping her foot
to the triumphant soul choons
blaring from her iPod.

Even softened through earphones
this one's Okeh:
"Oh yeah! Oh yeah!"

I picture myself
out on the floor:
spinning, twisting, turning.
The intricate steps of my feet,
the bass, the brass, the beat.

As a teenager
I didn't think about it,
just did it.

The Column Inches

i.m. Mary Millington (1945-1979)

It's not the screwing,
it's the being screwed;
never being yourself,
always being
what they want you to be —
even when
you don't know what that is;
the cold starts,
the broken hearts
splashed across
acres of gloss,
and all the while
remembering
to smile.

There But For the Grace of Bauhaus

The beige vomit
trailed down her front
sits vivid
against the black
of her coat.
Night buses
are indeed
a fantasy world.
The spatters
on her faux fur collar
smize.
Though she is fierce,
unrepentant
and glorious
in her drunkenness,
the puke in her hair
makes it difficult
to commit.
The stranger
sat next to me
must think the same
for she smiles

and we both laugh.
I stand for my stop
and she whispers,
"Get home safe."
The Goth
heaves into a newspaper.
David Cameron's face
looks appalled.

WPC Lucy Sheridan

As the Sixties swung,
she was one of many
whose face pressed
to the shop window.
Porn was a way
of paying the bills.
The *joie de vivre*
came from charlie
and good copy.
Constantly exposed,
yet always hidden,
she left four suicide notes.
One blonde police woman,
nicknamed Mary Millington
since the whole station
saw *The Playbirds*,
read them all, then
gathered them up
in a plain brown envelope.

Black Echoes

When I hugged Little Lorna — 'Little' 'cos she had a shorter afro and smaller attributes than Big Lorna — when I hugged Little Lorna close at the school disco, it was to Lovers Rock. Lovers Rock: that's Philly soul-kissing Jamdown sounds and teetering round Ridley Road on platform soles with a 'fro pick stuck in her do. Part of my growing up, and the city's (and so the country's too), was a sound drawn from many places, but a sound all England's own.

"I'm In Love With a Dreadlocks" sang Lorna into my ear as we rocked gently. At that, she rubbed my close-cropped barnet. At that, we laughed, and that's how it was. Even at school we could see that 'black' in a song could mean 'poor' anywheres: Kingston, Detroit, Memphis, even here in London. Hear in London. We didn't need sociology lessons to draw this lesson, which is just as well 'cos we had no sociology lessons, just hard knocks, hard times and hard cheese.

Even now, people find it strange that '70s English kids spent the money grafted from paper rounds, playground shpieling and Sunday market stalling on reggae. But reggae was the soundtrack to our no future, no ball games, no more heroes anymore. We heard it everywhere. It kept the prog-loving posh kids well away from us;

not that Hackney had an abundance of posh kids, or progress.

Lovers isn't even what I liked — not that any of us were averse to loving, there was just precious little. My choons were serious Joe Gibbs sevens on Crazy Joe, Town and Country, Heavy Duty. But what sort of girl is going to rub it up to 'Heavy Manners', 'Cool Out Son', 'No Bones For The Dogs'? I's a serious t'ing. And even if Little Lorna was also kissing up my top spar behind the bins, isn't it right that chinas should share? There was always Lois, Lorraine or Loretta. And as for Lovers? I've seen cheating, beating and stabbing plenty time, been part and party to all, but never then nor since to soooo sweet a beat.

The Story of Dalston

Newton Dunbar ran the Four Aces,
a pioneering club in Dalston;
not in the West End *fasharn* sense
but in real people's music sense —
reggae, soul, lovers, rave from the Sixties,
the Four Aces was home to them all.

When Hackney Council knocked down
his club, developers built plush flats
next to the Tube station
the Council had been promising us
since 1975 —
the kind no one local can afford.

Newton was asked
what's on the site of his club now?
Kissing his teeth in that Dalston way of old,
"Dem name a block after me," he conceded.
And how do you feel about that?
"One day *it* will be knocked down."

New Boots and Panties

We stayed in the pub, election night.
There were a few of us: the guv'nor,
the usual lads, some of the ever-popular
drunk sorts and the feisty Welsh barmaid.
By the time we clocked red London was sinking
we were tossing back the drinks,
less for the fun of it and more to lose the taste.
The jukebox took a beatin' too —
reggae and punk. Songs from our yoof.
'Babylon's Burning', I remember that all right.
'Beasley Street' was my choice.
We were up at the bar reciting along:
"Keith Joseph smiles and a baby dies…"
The Welsh girl asked who he was.
In honesty, the lilt of her voice deserved
a better answer. "He just moved in," I told her.
"You'll be hearing a lot about him."
Come the weekend she caught me by the elbow.
"I looked that Keith Joseph up," she said.
"He seems like a proper cunt."

My Nietzschean Overcoming of Culture

That there is
a 'Whole Foods Market'
in Stoke Newington
was pointed out to me
by my lovely girlfriend,
who cares about such things.

I could never set foot there
for fear someone I know
would see and shame me.

But because I love her so,
I go and buy her
soya milk and salad
and face softener
at the branch in Soho —
far from where I live.

Moshiach is Coming and He Doesn't Like My Kitchen

When the heart attack hits,
I wonder what my last sight will be:
drowning in blue eyes,
face down in goulash,
hair clogging the plughole?

Perhaps on my medically-sanctioned perambulation:
fallen leaves, a flock taking the wing,
a man picking up dog poop?
(Please not the latter!)

Darling, for everything,
I'm sorry.
Loving you, finally,
is more important
than being right.

Cooling the Scene

Broken glass sticks to my soles
as I step over another used condom
lying limp on Fleur de Lys Street.

A spray of hair is caught
in the chain-link fence;
strands are blown across the path.

A crushed, stained tissue edges
a puddle of blood.
The blood is fresh. I am not.

The Horror of Your Daughter's New Boyfriend Turning up Wearing Green Suede Cuban Heels

If that's not enough he's also sporting an open-necked white shirt —
wide enough that you see his nipples. It fair cuts a dash,
though, all in all, it's way too Errol Flynn. My troublesome daughter's
friend
looks me in the eye and rolls hers clockwise from quarter to
to half past, then peers at his chest before leaning close and whispering,
"His nipples are saying *Love me.*"
I differ and suggest they're rather saying
I would go out tonight but I haven't got a stitch to wear.

The conversation is awkward ~ my face has said it all ~ but I can see
an effort being made, and if he's doing that to please the girl
he can't be so bad. Her friends chip in with jokes and stories
to help us meet on middle ground. Beer makes company amiable,
and concord established I'm thinking he'll reconsider the shoes in
future.
Mid-joke, he mistakenly lifts and drains my pint. My face moves from
1950s disapproving dad to medieval.
Later that week a shirt is torn in the laundry, toast falls on suede, butter
side down.

The Woman She Was Supposed to Be

It was a present I gave her on her 21st.
Soon after she turned sober.
That bottle of champagne
sat in her fridge year on year.

When asked why she kept it,
she told me:
so long as it remained unopened
she was doing okay.

That made sense to me.
I'm glad what I gave her
was a measure of her strength.

Surviving

"He did a Gloria Gaynor:
walked out the door,
he wasn't welcome after that.
Six years and gone —
didn't even pack a bag.
After that I stopped drinking.
Not for good, but for a month;
just so I wouldn't phone
or text or crumble.
Look at these hands: steady.
Look at these eyes: clear.
He left for someone
who drank more than me."

Epsolutely

Epsom, let me tell you about Epsom.

The first time I met the parents of my girlfriend Alexis
they put on extra-posh accents to impress.
They were lovely and far posher than me —
it only took one *Ello, luverly to meet you*
for them to realise they'd over-invested;
but by then they couldn't back down.
Alexis whispered that they weren't normally that posh
and all she'd told them about me was I was lovely.
But they knew, that I knew, that they knew, that I knew,
that they knew, that I knew, that they knew, that I knew, that...

Epsom, let me tell you about Epsom.

Bin men pick up rubbish bags
with their pinky fingers daintily extended;
John Nettles is the law and the starlings sing
"You're beautiful, you're beautiful..."
in Epsom, let me tell you about Epsom.

I bought my girl chocolates.

There were only Conscious Chocolates, Green & Black's
and Seeds of Change in the pristine shops ~
middle-class chocolates with centres such as
'the better part of town', 'a good college' and 'a bit of rough' ~
in Epsom, let me tell you about Epsom.

There are no coincidences but sometimes
the pattern is more obvious
in Epsom, let me tell you about Epsom.

Alexis had a Porsche, in *not red, dahling; scarlet.*
She'd motor to Marks and Spencer, the Downs
and country pubs for lunch.
On our first outing she squeezed me in
and sped off in a polite cough of dust.
A few miles in, she remarked worriedly
that the car seemed to be dragging to the left.
She drove a bit further, then pulled over.
She walked around the sportster but could not find fault.
Again we drove and again she said the car was not right.
I asked her how many fat blokes she'd had in there before?

I got the train back from

Epsom, let me tell you about Epsom.

Red Sky at Night

On the aftermath of the London riots, Tuesday 9th August 2011

The gentry are coming —
with brooms!
Not to clean up the town,
but to sweep us
under the carpet.

Kosher Village

On the manor it's said:
a man who's not had
a heart attack by forty
is saying his wife can't cook.
And who can live with such shame?
See me at Maggie's bar,
at the meet of the going up
and coming down. We like
a bit of a larf, always *at, at, at*.
See a picture of yourself reflected
in the pool of your pint —
laugh or you'll go under.
It's your round goes around.
For years, the tracksuit blokes
have a grand changing hands
but never spent. I may walk away,
briskly even, but I will never run
from Stamford Hill,
where the heimishe are frum.

The Daily Grind

It's not that I'm sipping coffee
where once costermongers
swigged mugs of tea —
things change, we know that,
hope for it even —
but that the dreams they had
and I strive for still,
that they amount to nothing, as do we.

That never changes.
The more the tamping,
the more bitter the brew.
What really bites the cupcake
is that even the little we have,
the bastards feel entitled to that too.

I Don't <3 the Walk of Shame

The lager did sparkle,
but come darkness
the cocktails were cocked
and that girl's neckline
wasn't all that plunged.

There was dancing
and singing;
now a song you don't know
but know you don't like
is stuck in your head;

it plays to the rhythm
of your teetering steps.
Both shoes:
that's a plus at least.

Could the face that peers back
from shop window reflections
be the same one that last night
smiled and joked,
kissed and was kissed?

Yes, you got her number;
if only you could read it.
Saturday night tasted like life itself.
This cold Sunday morning
tastes of nothing at all.

The Bird Cage

She was saying we don't communicate,
that I don't really listen,
that she wasn't sure what she really wants.
But I wasn't paying attention;

I was hungover.
I was hungover and it was a hot day —
a hungover fat bloke on a hot day
ain't no sunshine.

When I should have been listening
I was too busy sweating,
feeling thirsty and imagining
a cold bottle of Lucozade —

one of those cold,
straight-from-the-corner-shop-fridge ones
with glass dimples
and a run of condensation down the side.

From the amber of Lucozade
it's a short stomach turn to lager

and that John Cooper Clarke line
'people turn to poison quick as lager turns to piss.'

The beads of sweat predominant on my forehead,
her talking, the drunk scrunching
of an empty crisp packet in a clammy hand
again and again and again —

meanwhile on Mongo,
Ming the Merciless hatches plots.

Effingham

I feel numb, or rather
don't feel,
staring blankly
through the train window.

Now there's no more
me and her
I'll not be making
this journey again.

Sunshine dapples the woods,
bluebells crowd the shade —
her eyes the same
deep blue.

The lushness of a spring field.
A hawk circles, swoops,
tears at a leveret.
It is beautiful.

The Coriolanus Effect

For the East End tourist industry

Come
ye learned,
ye loquacious,
ye lost.

Walk a pentagram
around ego,
erudition,
experience.

Our shuls,
mosques
and homes
be yours.

Our murdered
laid bare,
our slums
still teem,
our souls sold.

As for us,
we marvel as
our own effluvia
swirls
widdershins.

Fight For This Love

Two Shoreditch fashion blondes
are strutting it
down a windblown street.
"I slept with Toby this weekend,"
ripped tights tells her mate.
"Did he ask?"
enquires ironic t-shirt,
posh scarf, sunglasses, languidly.
"Yes," replies
the lucky, lucky girl.

We'll Take a Cup o' Kindness Yet

The first drunks are early,
and so the fireworks;
could be the Old Bill
gunning another man down.
They've already sped past —
sirens, lights — giving us an anthem.

Outside the Rochester
the girls are singing
last year's pop songs.
The prettiest one is puking.
Bring it up, girl. New Year,
it's better out than in.

The Wells

Including lines lifted from Billy Bragg's 'Levi Stubbs' Tears'

In the recriminations of break up,
the lament with the horn section wins.
The burst of hurt, punch of sorrow, flourish of self
bruise soul no matter how fabulous your chassis.
When the world falls apart some things stay in place.
Levi Stubbs' tears run down his face.

Before the Blues put the swagger in a fellow
and the sass to a woman, this was a song sang long.
Norman Whitfield and Barratt Strong
are here to make right everything that's wrong.
Holland and Holland and Lamont Dozier too
are here to make it all okay with you.

Even poured on a drowning man,
you don't miss your water till your well runs dry.
Floods, drought, drinks tossed in your face:
when the world falls apart some things stay in place,
Levi Stubbs' tears.

Steiner

She'd read the reviews and wanted to go.
I was keen to encourage.
How often does your girlfriend want to see a war film?
And so, we ended up at the *Rio*.
It's one of those arty cinemas that does film festivals,
doesn't recognise a union or pay the living wage.
Still, a war film — a date and a war film.

You'll have seen the film. You'll know it's majestic.
The rumblings of bombardment resonate throughout.
Halfway through, with my arm around her,
I pulled closer to see what she made of it.
The reflected light of the screen shone on
tears running down the dark of her face.

"Sakina, are you okay? What's wrong?"
"Hitler's generals... they're leaving him," she sobbed.
The shock of her words fired though me. I blew up,
started yelling and profusely swearing.
My own girlfriend, sympathising with Hitler!

In front, some puffed up Parma ham-eating puffin

interjected and told me to be quiet.
I grabbed him by the lapel and punched him
square on the nose. He went down.
Me and the girl have never spoken thereafter.

Since, the same scene unfolds time and time again.
The same situation, different words but the same collapse
unfolding time and time again. Others find it amusing,
but this meme of my downfall, me ranting and raving,
plays through my life again and again and again.

My Friends, the Poets

My local knows I write.
Every proper pub has its share of characters;
the bloke shot by the Taliban,
the girl who fell asleep having sex in the toilet.
We're not the chattering classes,
more gossip and dirty jokes.

Cockney, Yiddische, Gammon and Yard
is the well I dip my pen in.
We like a turn of phrase, an inventive curse,
when somebody says nothing but everything.
The Up-themselves and the Bore we've no time for,
yet there's a true appreciation for the form.

I'm often asked about poets: Luke Kennard,
Ian Duhig, Clare Pollard… do I know them?
What are they like? The library takes a hit
and there's a second appreciative read
when my reply is, "You'd love 'em,
they're a scumbag just like us."

NOTES

'Hoxton Market Forces'
In 2014 Catherine Yates wanted to drop a piano from Poplar flats, the Balfron Tower, 'as part of a community workshop to explore how sound travels,' and was stopped by local opposition.

'Kuu'
Kuu: moon in Finnish.

'Ryoko Naitoh Writes a Song'
クソガキ — Kusogaki / brat.

'Out of the Blue'
Ermine Street is the Roman road that runs up Stamford Hill.

'Bidaaye'
Bidaaye: goodbye in Sylheti.

'Mudies Mood'
I once dumped a girl for stepping on my 7 of The Drifter, and I'd do it again!

'WPC Lucy Sheridan'
WPC Lucy Sheridan was Mary Millington's role in *The Playbirds*, 1978.

'Moshiach is Coming and He Doesn't Like My Kitchen'
Just a shmek before the main bris.

'Epsolutely'
I used to have a middle-class girlfriend. I didn't hate her for it; I
hated myself.

'The Bird Cage'
Flash Gordon's enemy Ming the Merciless is the ruler of the planet
Mongo.

'Effingham'
Well you would, wouldn't you?

'My Friends, the Poets'
Gammon is cant spoken by Irish Travellers. Yard is Jamaican slang.

MANY OF THESE POEMS WERE WRITTEN IN THE FOLLOWING PUBS:

the Betsey Trotwood, Mascara Bar, the Golden Heart, Doc Holliday's, the Paradise Bar and Grill, the Niagra, the Angel, the Mad Dog in the Fog, the Derby Arms, the Troublesome Daughter, the Oxford Bar, the Pride of Spitalfields, the Jolly Butchers (as was), the Owl and the Pussycat (as was), the Hole in the Wall, the Maurice Gosfield, Dick's Bar (home of the espresso martini), the International Bar, the Pillars of Hercules, the Wanker and Joke, wherever Geri Lynn was working (miss you x), the Town of Ramsgate, the Prospect of Whitby, Korova Milk Bar, the Globe (hello to Anna Massey), Nell of Old Drury, the Slaughtered Lamb, the High Maintenance Girlfriend, the Girl Who Was Death, the Queen Vic, the Blarney Stone (Aileen Cho, you're the business), the Poetry Establishment, the Ship and Shovel, the Sherlock Holmes, the Albio , the Wally Dug, the Wellesley, the Sir George Robey, the Inebriated Gremlin ('That was very, very dirty' – Mrs Peel), the Daniel Defoe, the Mucky Pup, Sowici's (the best dinner in town), the Green Man (the landlord's daughter!), The Ellangowan Hotel, The Winchester Club, the Terry and June, the Cat and Mouse, the Admiral Benbow, the John Snow, Fillet O'Soul ('there's a honky coming uptown'), Mars Bar, Austerity Measures, the Midnight Bell.

If you enjoyed this book you may also like Jackie Collins' *Deadly Embrace*.